MW01490032

~FROM~

~DATE~

Healing Quotes

(Volume One)
Words with Power Series

Copyright © 2009, Eddie Lawrence
ISBN 13: 978-0-9790830-3-7
ISBN 10: 0-9790830-3-6
All Rights Reserved

First Printing, September 2009

Riverworn Publishing
(A Division of Riverworn, Inc.)
760 County Rd 27
Florence, AL 35634
www.Riverworn.com

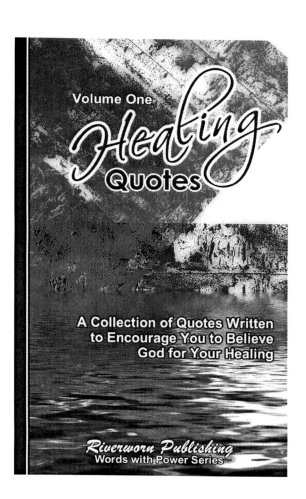

Volume One

Healing Quotes

A Collection of Quotes Written
to Encourage You to Believe
God for Your Healing

Riverworn Publishing
Words with Power Series

HEALING QUOTES
Volume One

PREFACE

This first volume compilation of Healing Quotes has been put together with the prayer and desire to help and encourage people in their battle with sickness whether in body or soul. It is also compiled as a resource to be used by people who minister to the sick.

Let it serve as a box of ammo for battling sickness in any of its forms. Words are extremely powerful. God's Word is most powerful. In this book, you will read words from God and men alike that address the subject of "healing." You will notice a variety of names throughout the book representing different streams of thought and approach in regard to healing. Some of them you may recognize; others you may not. Most of the people whose names appear have written or ministered in the areas of prayer and/or healing.

Of course, these quotes are in no way meant to replace God's Word but rather to reinforce the fact that every good and perfect gift, including healing, comes from our Father above.

Read them, meditate upon them, and use them to encourage your soul and others in the battle against sickness and disease.

It is my prayer that the healing presence of God Himself will be released into your life and that you will prosper and be in good health in body, soul, and spirit.

Blessings,
Eddie Lawrence

Riverworn Publishing
Words with Power Series

We may safely assume that God wants the best for us and that only He knows what that is. However, we are not to remain passive in the midst of discomfort, disease, and pain. We are to ask! He will either give us what we ask or something better. We must not use the "will of God" to shield us against faith. Armed with the Word of God, which is a statement of the will of God, we are to ask in faith.

-Jack Taylor,
The Word of God with Power

As we wait upon the Lord, we are going to be renewed in our strength (like the eagle). The word "renew" in this context, means to "exchange" as if taking off old clothes and putting on brand new clothes. This literally means to "experience an invigorated, restorative rest." ...It is a rest that restores our spirit, soul, and body....We exchange our weakness for His power.

-Leif Hetland,
Soaring As Eagles

Healing prayer is part of the normal Christian life. It should not be elevated above any other ministry in the community of faith, nor should it be undervalued; rather it should be kept in proper balance. It is simply a normal aspect of what it means to live under the reign of God.

– Richard J. Foster,
Prayer

People continually ask me, "What can I do to receive my miracle?" "Nothing," I tell them. Healing is not a result of what we can do. It is a result of what Christ has *already done*.

-Benny Hinn,
This Is Your Day For A Miracle

Embracing a belief system that requires no faith is dangerous. It is contrary to the nature of God and all that the Scriptures declare....His promises by nature challenge our intellect and expectations.

– Bill Johnson,
When Heaven Invades Earth

May we never treat the sacrifice of Christ in a manner that would deprive and empty the cross of its power. The overwhelming grace of God is freely given to enable each of us to embrace Christ, making it possible to receive all that He accomplished for us in His death upon the cross and His resurrection from the dead. Because He is victorious over death, hell, and the grave, we can walk victorious in this world.

– Bobby Conner,
The Cross

The key to receiving healing for your body is in knowing Christ, not only as the One Who healed the multitudes two thousand years ago, but as your healer. Divine healing is not a doctrine; it is God's very life flowing into you through Christ, by His spirit within you!

– Morris Cerullo,
Christ, Your Healer

Sin in the soul and sickness in the body both bear witness to the power of Satan, and "the Son of God was manifested that He might destroy the works of the Devil" (I John 3:8).

– Andrew Murray,
Divine Healing

Every promise of Scripture is a writing of God, which may be pleaded before Him with this reasonable request: "Do as Thou hast said." The Creator will not cheat His creature who depends upon His truth; and, far more, the Heavenly Father will not break His word to His own child.

– Charles H. Spurgeon

The writer (of Proverbs) also wrote how a crushed spirit will affect a person. "A man's spirit sustains him in sickness, but a crushed spirit who can bear?" (Proverbs 18:14). A vibrant spirit helps a person through great difficulties, but a crushed spirit has a crippling effect in all areas of life.

– Derek Prince,
God's Remedy for Rejection

Hebrews 13:8 (KJV) tells us "Jesus Christ is the same yesterday, and today, and forever." We can't say that healing passed away with the early church, which some people teach. What Jesus did in the days He was walking on the earth, He will also do for you today. If He was healing people then, He is certainly about the business of healing people today.

– Joyce Meyer,
Be Healed in Jesus' Name

If the age of miracles is past, no one could be born again because the new birth is the greatest miracle a person can experience.

– T.L. Osborn,
Healing the Sick

He *restoreth my soul* can have another meaning. Moffatt translates it to read, "He revives life in me." Like a watch, the human spirit can just run down. We lose our drive and push. We become less willing to attempt the difficult. We are crusaders no longer. Like squeezing the juice from an orange and leaving just the pulp, life has a way of squeezing the spirit out of a person.... And God has the power and the willingness to breathe a new breath of life into one who has lost.

-Charles L. Allen,
God's Psychiatry

We may be thankful to God for having given us doctors. Their vocation is one of the most noble, for a large number of them seek truly to do, with love and compassion, all they are able to alleviate the evils and sufferings which burden humanity as a result of sin.... Nevertheless it is Jesus Himself who is always the first, the best, the greatest Physician.

– Andrew Murray,
Divine Healing

We can rely on the mercy of God. When we or those around us have a need, count on the mercy of God. We should not count on our rights as much as on the mercy of God. The Lord doesn't owe us anything, but He always responds to cries for mercy.

– Mahesh Chavda,
The Hidden Power of the
Believer's Touch

We ought to live every day as though we've come out of another world into this world -- but with the power of that world still upon us. We should live and speak and move in that power, and have our whole being in Jesus Christ!

- John Wesley

Was there any failure when Jesus laid hands on the blind man and he wasn't healed the first time? Of course not! Jesus was doing everything the Father was telling Him to do, because that's how He lived (John 5:19). So why did God the Father temporarily cause a partial healing through Jesus at that time? To teach us that obedience is the key, and that we shouldn't give up, but continue to seek God for directions as to the next step.

– Joy Dawson, Some of the Ways of God in Healing

Although the world is full of suffering, it is also full of the overcoming of it.

- Helen Keller

God wants to show you to sweep away everything else, and dare to believe that Word. If you allow anything to come in between you and that Word, it will poison your whole system, and you will have no hope. One bit of unbelief against that Word is poison. It is like the devil putting a spear into you.

– Smith Wigglesworth

Speak to the mountain, speak to the storm, speak to the fig tree, speak to the disease, speak to the finances, and speak to the demons. In the presence of God, you see what He is doing; you learn His word; and then, as His representative on earth, you speak the command just as Jesus did.

– Pat Robertson,
Miracles Can Be Yours Today

We need to live *from God* instead of living *for God*. You cannot perform His promises. Healing is a promise not a problem. His promises are realized through faith and trust. We keep thinking we are to achieve something for God when what we need is to learn is how to receive something from God. When we learn to do this, we will wear out the enemy through our rest and experience God performing His promises for us, in us, to us, and through us.

-Leif Hetland

Very solemnly He declared that every disciple of His would have to bear his cross (Matthew 16:24), but He never taught one sick person to resign himself to be sick. Everywhere Jesus healed the sick, everywhere He dealt with healing as one of the graces belonging to the kingdom of heaven.

– Andrew Murray,
Divine Healing

God cares as much about the body as he does the soul, as much about the emotions as he does the spirit. The redemption that is in Jesus is total, involving every aspect of the person—body, soul, will, mind, emotions, spirit.

– Richard J. Foster,
Prayer

Jesus is the same yesterday, today, and forever! His love for the lost has never diminished.... God has never compromised and has never withdrawn love or faith. He is Savior, Healer, Deliverer, and King.

– Patricia King,
Light Belongs in the Darkness

The nature of God's promises in Scripture is that each promise contains within itself the power to perform the promise that it contains. It reproduces like a seed. It is God's Word. It is alive. It is powerful. To access its explosive potential, we plant it in our hearts and surround it with faith like a farmer planting a crop. This is where it grows.

- Eddie Lawrence,
Sermon Seedbed

If we believe only what we can see with our natural eyes, we will fail. Until we see the *invisible*, we will not do the *impossible*.

– Jack Taylor,
Victory Over the Devil

Because of what He endured on the cross, the Lord fully understands the pain and suffering we experience. "For we have not an high priest which cannot be touched with the feelings of our infirmities" (Heb. 4:15, KJV).

-Benny Hinn,
This Is Your Day For A Miracle

We have multiple-choice definitions of truth, different versions of Scripture, a variety of theological perspectives, and no power. Hospitals are filling up and churches are closing down.... Theology is meant to help us discover God and live in the abundance of Christ and His resurrection power. Primitive Christianity means a return to the original roots of supernatural Christianity, practiced in simple, uncomplicated ways.

-Graham Cooke,
A Divine Confrontation

Healing, even by faith, is not always instantaneous. There are "miracles" and "gifts of healing," the one sudden and stupendous, the other simple and probably gradual.

– A. B. Simpson,
The Gospel of Healing

I'm sure some who read these lines have faced or are even now facing the impossible in terms of what God has called them to do and to be…. The enemy's blow is calculated to maim or to crush—to stop them right in their tracks. But God's message to His own is ever the same: "My power and the strength that I give you are sufficient. Call upon it, ask for it, see if I will not cause all grace to abound toward you!"

-Leanne Payne,
Restoring The Christian Soul

The blood of Jesus, infused with the power to heal, is still as active today as ever. In fact, His blood will be active forever.

– Chuck D. Pierce &
Rebecca Wagner Systema,
Prayers That Outwit the Enemy

But we come against disease as Jesus came against it, not denying its reality, but driving it out as the Master did, healing it, the health and life of the Son of God displacing it. It is not error to say disease is; it is the truth, acknowledge it. It takes faith to destroy it.

-E.W. Kenyon,
The Limitlessness of Faith

Faith comes for healing in the same way it comes for salvation—by hearing the Word of God.

– Gloria Copeland

Everything the devil introduced to men and women was undone by Jesus at the cross, which of course includes sickness. Jesus, the new Adam, came to restore us, to reproduce his new nature in us—which touches every part of our being.

– John Wimber,
Power Healing

When you sow a seed, you don't dig it up every morning to see if it's come to pass. If you do, your seed will never come up. You've got to plant it, commit it to the earth, and let it alone. It's up to nature, God, to water it and see that it produces.... That's the way you do the Word of God.

– William Branham

Faith is that quality or power by which the things desired become the things possessed.

- Kathryn Kuhlman

Divine association with God is more than ten regiments of soldiers.

– Smith Wigglesworth

If you have the desire to be healed by God, then there is a God to heal you. Deep calls unto deep.

-William Branham

God wants us to be well!

But, God has more than one assembly line available to Him by which He delivers the finished product. Obviously, conditions must be met in order to receive from the Lord. A knowledge of the Father's love, faith in the completed work of the cross of Christ, and patient abiding in the Word of God are but a few of these essentials.

– Jim Goll,
The Healing Anointing

One might ask, "Does it matter how we think God feels towards us? ...." Have you ever thought about how much you react to other people based on how you perceive they must think of you?... Satan, who understands this, constantly reminds us of our sins against God so that we constantly feel God is angry or upset with us. By doing this he drives a wedge that keeps us from relating to a God who loves us so much.

– Kyle Searcy,
From Legalism to Love

The cult of humanism in our day has trained us to believe that we are quite adequate to be masters of our own destiny. Yet, not only did Jesus insist on the truth of our helplessness; He underscored it by telling us that this same helplessness applied equally to Him while He wore human flesh: "I can of mine own self do nothing: [He told His apostles,] The Father in me doeth the works." In this as in everything else, He was setting the pattern of perfect humanity.

– Catherine Marshall,
Adventures in Prayer

When you come to God through Jesus, you discover that you are already accepted. God has no second-class children. He does not just tolerate you. He loves you. He is interested in you. He cares for you.

– Derek Prince,
God's Remedy for Rejection

Man has a twofold nature. He is both a material and a spiritual being. And both natures have been equally affected by the Fall. His body is exposed to disease; his soul is corrupted by sin. How blessed, therefore, to find that the complete scheme of redemption includes both natures. It provides for the restoration of physical as well as the renovation of spiritual life!

— A. B. Simpson,
The Gospel of Healing

We have seen too much, we have tasted too much of the power of the age to come, we have drunk too deeply of the love of God to ever say again, "No, there isn't enough. That's all Jesus has. I'm sorry." No we will always say, "Go to Him. Eat and drink of Him. What we don't have, He has. Be desperate for Him. Have faith in Him. Love Him. Look into His eyes. His body and blood are enough for all who will receive Him."

– Rolland and Heidi Baker,
There Is Always Enough

Faith will work without prayer, but prayer will not work without faith. You can put your faith to work through prayer. "And the prayer of faith shall save the sick, and the Lord shall raise him up (James 5:15).

– Charles Capps.
Releasing the Ability of God

Prayer is not overcoming God's reluctance. It is laying hold of God's willingness.

- George Mueller

To learn how to believe that God hears us when we pray is a much greater blessing than is the healing itself, because then, the prayer of faith can be repeated ten thousand times, for ourselves and others, and thus our whole life is spent in obtaining the fulfillment of Divine Promises.

– F. F. Bosworth

We need to realize that the promises that overflow our Bibles will overflow into our own lives only as we appropriate them through prayer.

– Jim Cymbala,
Breakthrough Prayer

The purpose of God's promises is fulfillment. Why else would He have given them to us? Jesus used His knowledge of Scripture to overcome Satan in the wilderness. We can also take advantage of the Scripture made available to us to overcome Satan's attacks. When Satan attacks us with sickness or disease, use the Word as a weapon against him. The Word will always prevail.

– Mike Joyner,
Divine Health and Healing Principles

Today there is bread, there is life, there is health for every child of God through His all-powerful Word. The Word can drive every disease away from your body. It is your portion in Christ, Him who is our bread, our life, our health, our all in all.

– Smith Wigglesworh

The Lord is concerned about fulfilling our desires, but to do so He must pry our fingers off our lives and turn our hearts toward Him. Indeed, the reason we are alive is not to fulfill our desires but to become His worshipers.

– Francis Frangipane,
The Place of Immunity

The death of Christ destroys sin – the root of sickness. But it is the life of Jesus that supplies the source of health and life for our redeemed bodies. The body of Christ is the living fountain of all our vital strength.

– A. B. Simpson,
The Gospel of Healing

A car was made to run on gasoline, and it would not run properly on anything else. Now God designed the human machine to run on Himself. He Himself is the fuel our spirits were designed to burn, or the food our spirits were designed to feed on. There is no other.

– C. S. Lewis,
Mere Christianity

I respect doctors, and one reason is that they have grasped this eternal truth and are against sickness and for health. Consciously or unconsciously, they have a pretty good theology of healing. Sometimes I wish we Christians had such a good theology of healing. Then we might be less inclined to argue about whether it's God's will to heal or not."

- Oral Roberts

We don't have faith because we understand, but we understand because we have faith. In other words, it is imperative to accept and understand things without completely satisfying the intellect. When I read the Bible, I don't always understand what I am reading.... A normal Christian is one who obeys the revelations and promptings of the Holy Spirit without understanding.

– Bill Johnson,
The Supernatural Power of a
Transformed Mind

Because the Savior has overcome the devil, we have overcome the devil. His overcoming becomes our overcoming. As he substituted for us in death, now he substitutes for us in life. Just as we accepted his death for our *wickedness*, we now accept his life for our *weakness*.

– Jack Taylor,
Victory Over the Devil

Like many others I have discovered that, when praying for people with the laying on of hands, I sometimes detect a gentle flow of energy. I have found that I cannot make the flow of heavenly life happen, but I can stop it. If I resist or refuse to be an open conduit for God's power to come into a person, it will stop.

– Richard J. Foster,
Prayer

When a Christian shuns fellowship with other Christians, the devil smiles. When he stops studying the Bible, the devil laughs. When he stops praying, the devil shouts for joy.

- Corrie Ten Boom

In each of these statements (Matthew 19:26, Mark 9:23), we find the words "all things are possible." In the first passage, they are applied to God; in the second, they are applied to the one who believes. It is not too difficult, perhaps, to accept all things are possible to God. Can we equally accept that all things are possible to the one who believes? This is what Jesus told us.

– Derek Prince,
Faith to Live By

To live in heaven now is the normal Christian life (Ephesians 2:4-6). We are there now. If we are in Christ, we are presently seated at the right hand of the Father in the heavenly places. This is something that we must accept by faith, but faith is meant to give substance to the things hoped for; faith is meant to become a reality with substance.

– Rick Joyner,
The Morning Star Journal

There is a mighty lot of difference between saying prayers and praying.

- John G. Lake

Remember, God is love! God is in a good mood. God is for you, not against you. Jesus has done the work for you. On your report card in Heaven, you get the "A" that Jesus made instead of the "F" that you deserve. You are a winner! Learn to rest in who *He is* instead of struggling about who *you were*. Keep your eyes on Jesus.

-Leif Hetland

Everybody has to have testings. If you believe in Divine Healing you will surely be tested on the faith line. God cannot bring anyone into blessing and into full co-operation with Him except through testings and trials.

– Smith Wigglesworth

I live in the spirit of prayer. I pray as I walk about, when I lie down, and when I rise up. And the answers are always coming. Thousands of times have my prayers been answered. When once I am persuaded that a thing is right and for the glory of God, I go on praying for it until the answer comes. George Mueller never gives up.

– George Mueller

The way to pray for cancer ordinarily has two elements in it. One is the prayer part where we ask God to heal the cancer or we command the cancer cells to stop multiplying. This takes just a short time. Then comes the laying on of hands, which is like God's own radiation treatment. This part can take plenty of time. The longer the cancer is held in God's force-field, the more healing takes place. Sick cells die, while healthy cells take on added life.

– Francis McNutt

It (the word *persevere*) implies that there are times when we will not reach our spiritual goals unless we are stretched in ways others call severe or extreme. We don't go one mile; we go two....We are not wimps; we don't give up. We are soldiers who endure hardship. Even if we are knocked down, defeat is not final. We rise to fight another day. Surrender is not an option.

– Francis Frangipane,
This Day We Fight

The abundant life that Jesus promised to His disciples is found in this unseen realm. The display of His dominion through miracles and various supernatural expressions are all rooted in this heavenly world. We must access His world to change this one.

– Bill Johnson,
Dreaming With God

Even though Matthew 8:17 says, "That it might be fulfilled which was spoken by Isaiah the prophet saying, 'He Himself took our infirmities and bore our sicknesses,'" we still battle the curse of sickness from time to time. We must all appropriate, by faith, what Jesus did for us on the cross. And when we don't, we continue to experience some of the effects of the curse.

— Robert Morris,
The Blessed Life

When Jesus taught us to pray "will of God be done on Earth as it is in Heaven", he gave us the target at which we are to aim. There is no sickness in Heaven. Therefore, we should always rally in our own homes for those things that God has chosen for His. Each such victory gives us moments of what will ultimately become our state of being.

– Eddie Lawrence
Sermon Seedbed

Until the person seeking healing is sure from God's Word that it is God's will to heal him, he is trying to reap a harvest where there is no seed planted.

– F.F. Bosworth,
Christ the Healer

Your thoughts are powerful. They aren't just images and attitudes that lurk in your head; they determine who you are, and who you are going to become. Given this reality, shouldn't you make thinking the right kind of thoughts a top priority in your life?

– Joyce Meyer,
Battlefield of the Mind

Oh, let us believe in the name of Jesus! Was it not in the name of Jesus that perfect health was given to the impotent man? And were not these words: Thy faith hath saved thee, pronounced when the body was healed? Let us seek then to obtain divine healing.

– Andrew Murray,
Divine Healing

But God says He doesn't change. He is the same yesterday, today, and tomorrow. Why would He have done miracles for thousands of years and stop now? I know from experience that God does miracles and I firmly believe that He can do a miracle in your life today.

– Stormie Omartian,
Lord, I Want to Be Whole

Deep in our DNA is the nature of a King. He speaks to us from within our inner nature, and sometimes when we're under mounds of circumstantial rubble, "in all these things we overwhelmingly conquer" (Romans 8:37). We were made to rule!

– Dutch Sheets,
Authority in Prayer

The Bible teaches us in Mark, chapter 4, that the Word of God is seed. If you plant the seed of God's Word, you can reap a harvest of results; but you must plant the specific seed that you want. If you plant corn, you will reap corn. If you plant the Word for salvation in your heart, you will have faith to receive salvation. When you plant the Word concerning healing in your heart, you will reap the healing harvest.

– Gloria Copeland

Our experience... is that the person who receives a healing or deliverance no longer has a problem believing Jesus is alive. Often it goes beyond a believing – it's a knowing. Jesus is not just a memory, not just a great leader who lived 2,000 years ago. He lives!

– Francis McNutt

God's Word does not say, "Call unto me, and you will thereby be trained into the happy art of knowing how to be denied. Ask, and you will learn sweet patience by getting nothing." Far from it. But it is definite, clear and positive: "Ask, and it shall be given unto you."

- E. M. Bounds

Forgiving does not erase the bitter past. A healed memory is not a deleted memory. Instead, forgiving what we cannot forget creates a new way to remember. We change the memory of our past into a hope for our future.

- Lewis B. Smedes

In Jesus' day, the religious leaders finally concluded that His healings were happening but that they were done through the power of Satan. People will generally look for any explanation other than God.

– Don Stewart,
Only Believe

It is sobering to realize that if we have unbelief in our hearts, we can read the Scriptures, but we will fail to hear the voice of the Father giving testimony to who He is in its verses. Unbelief literally blinds and deafens our hearts to His voice, thereby effectively blocking the most powerful thing in the universe from being active in and through us.

– Bill Johnson,
Release the Power of Jesus

Jesus declared that the least amount of faith that he could give was greater and mightier than the largest amount of the power of the devil.

-Kathryn Kuhlman

The good news is, it can happen to you. You can be restored to health. You can be set free. Don't put it off. Get help.... You need to forgive everyone you've been angry with or bitter toward. And then you need to forgive yourself, knowing that God Himself forgives you. Then, when you've found someone to pray with you and stand against the devil, commanding his demons to leave you alone in the name of Jesus Christ, you will be restored and delivered.

– James Robison

I want to tell you, "There's more! God has more to pour out on you! You can have more of the anointing...more of Him! But in order to receive it, you must let Him have more of you!"

– Randy Clark,
Lighting Fires

If it is not God's will for you to be well, it would be wrong for you to seek recovery even through natural means.

— T. L. Osborn,
Healing the Sick

There is healing through the blood of Christ and deliverance for every captive. God never intended His children to live in misery because of some affliction that comes directly from the devil. A perfect atonement was made at Calvary. I believe that Jesus bore my sins, and I am free from them all. I am justified from all things if I dare believe. He Himself took our infirmities and bare our sicknesses; and if I dare believe, I can be healed.

–Smith Wigglesworth

If Jesus occasionally took time to heal or exorcise people, we certainly can expect that we also, upon occasion, must take time. When some sick people are not healed through prayer, it may simply be because we haven't prayed long enough to bring the healing to completion.

– Francis McNutt

Taken together, these verses, (Luke 13:11-13, Matthew 9:32-33) show that demons have the power to cause sickness and disease. While we cannot infer that every sickness is brought on by some demonic oppression, these passages demonstrate that inducing physical infirmities is one of the weapons demons use to destroy an individual.

– Bill & Michael French,
The Remedy

When we feed our spirit man the eternal Word of God, then our spirit man will begin to crave more of the eternal. The content of the eternal Word bears witness to the spirit of a man. A man begins to sense the similarity between his deepest yearning and what he senses when he hears or reads the Word of God. It is like a letter sent to him from back home. So feast on the Word in order to know more of what is going on at Father's house.

– Eddie Lawrence,
Sermon Seedbed

I have laid hands on people with appendicitis in almost every part of the world and never knew of a case not instantly healed, even when doctors were on the premises.

– Smith Wigglesworth (who had previously been healed from appendicitis)

When we remember what God has done, it's as though we take the seed of a particular miracle, deposit it in a new environment, and another miracle takes place.

– Bill Johnson,
Release the Power of Jesus

To put an *if* into God's promise, where God has put none, is tantamount to charging God with being insincere. It is like saying, "O God, if thou art in earnest in making these promises, grant us the blessing we pray for."

– Charles Finney

Divine healing is not something that's just a totem pole, or a hocus-pocus. It's a Divine Truth, written in the Word of God, and confirmed by the Holy Spirit. It's not limited to any denomination, people, creed, or color; it's to whosoever will. Just like salvation, it is a product of a finished work that we receive by faith in the great vicarious suffering and triumphant resurrection of the Lord Jesus.

– William Branham

Always remember, Jesus knows every pain you feel. He hears your cries and His heart is full of mercy for you. In His sovereign grace, that moment will come when He will say, "This is your day for a miracle!"

-Benny Hinn,
This Is Your Day For A Miracle

MAY GOD BLESS YOU WITH HIS GRACE AND MAY YOU BE HAPPY, HEALTHY, AND HOLY!